THE WORKBOOK OF HUMAN SUPERPOWERS

This book is based on the Essence Glossary ™
ESSENCEGLOSSARY.COM
Porrata, M. & Pretti-Frontczak, K. (2014).
Essence Glossary ™. Akron, Ohio.

ISBN 978-1523996261
Original Library of Congress Control Number: 2016908751

Soul Publishing Group ™

ABOUT THE ESSENCE GLOSSARY

The ESSENCE GLOSSARY ™ is a resource designed to promote social-emotional awareness and intelligence. The glossary is a listing, with simple definitions, of 32 social-emotional attributes we feel are essential to learning and promoting well-being in our homes, schools, and communities. In fact, many of these attributes have been independently tested, and are already the basis for educational and community health education interventions and initiatives across the country and the world.

The glossary is a free resource and is available in English, as well as other languages. Copies of the translated glossary may be downloaded at: http://www.essenceglossary.com/foreign-language/

DEDICATION

For my daughters, Serena and Camille
For my parents, Mari Fernández -Préstamo and Santiago Porrata-Doria

Mayra

With gratitude to my Mom and Dad, who lovingly modeled for me
the superpowers of advocacy, humor, and a love of learning.

Kristie

How to use this book:

COLOR ⟶

REVIEW DEFINITION ⟶

KINDNESS
helpful, generous, and
unconditional approach
to self and others

REFLECT & JOURNAL ⟶

HOW CAN I GROW & NURTURE THIS POWER IN:

MYSELF?

OTHERS?

MY COMMUNITY?

TABLE OF CONTENTS

TABLE OF CONTENTS

Adaptability

ADAPTABILITY
openness to changing conditions

HOW CAN I GROW & NURTURE THIS POWER IN:

MYSELF?

OTHERS?

MY COMMUNITY?

Advocacy

ADVOCACY
encourages multiple views by promoting choice, expression of opinions, and equal rights

HOW CAN I GROW & NURTURE THIS POWER IN:

MYSELF?

OTHERS?

MY COMMUNITY?

Appreciation

APPRECIATION
recognizes the inherent
qualities within self, others, and
everyday experiences

HOW CAN I GROW & NURTURE THIS POWER IN:

MYSELF?

OTHERS?

MY COMMUNITY?

ATTENTION
purposefully and selectively
directs the mind

HOW CAN I GROW & NURTURE THIS POWER IN:

MYSELF?

OTHERS?

MY COMMUNITY?

15

Bravery

BRAVERY
overcomes fear and
uncertainty to take action

HOW CAN I GROW & NURTURE THIS POWER IN:

MYSELF?

OTHERS?

MY COMMUNITY?

Charity

CHARITY
shares one's time, talents, and resources

HOW CAN I GROW & NURTURE THIS POWER IN:

MYSELF?

OTHERS?

MY COMMUNITY?

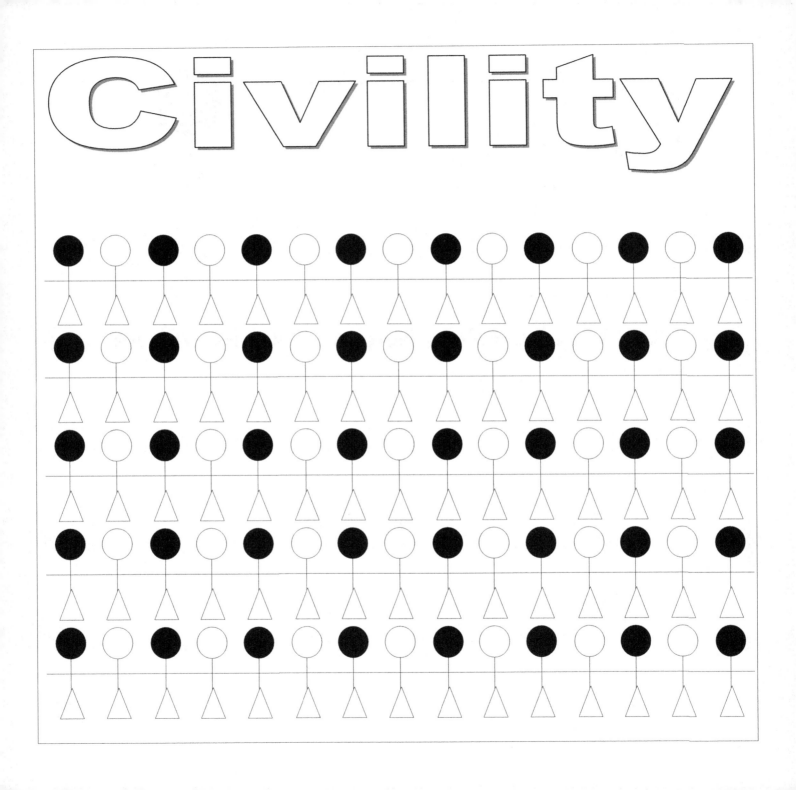

Civility

CIVILITY
uses respectful words and
actions towards others

HOW CAN I GROW & NURTURE THIS POWER IN:

MYSELF?

OTHERS?

MY COMMUNITY?

Compassion

COMPASSION
recognizes human need
and is motivated to address

HOW CAN I GROW & NURTURE THIS POWER IN:

MYSELF?

OTHERS?

MY COMMUNITY?

Creativity

CREATIVITY
constructs, connects, and
adapts information in new ways

HOW CAN I GROW & NURTURE THIS POWER IN:

MYSELF?

OTHERS?

MY COMMUNITY?

25

Curiosity

CURIOSITY
interested and willing to
explore and discover

HOW CAN I GROW & NURTURE THIS POWER IN:

MYSELF?

OTHERS?

MY COMMUNITY?

Discernment

DISCERNMENT
considers relevant information to make sound decisions

HOW CAN I GROW & NURTURE THIS POWER IN:

MYSELF?

OTHERS?

MY COMMUNITY?

Empathy

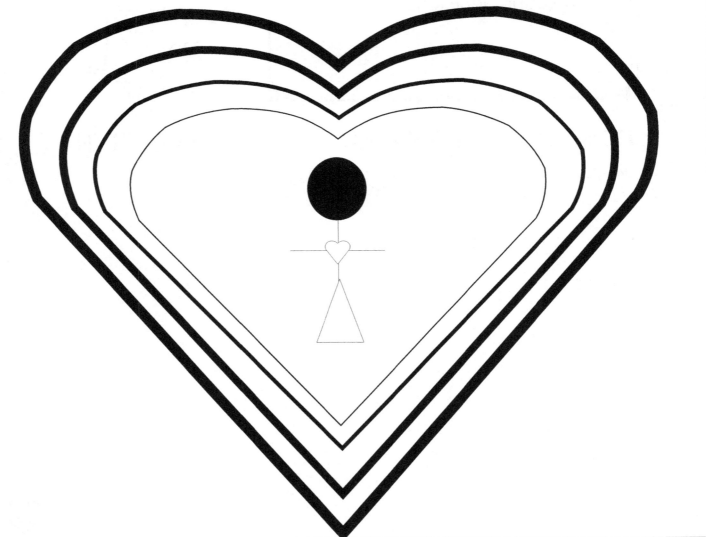

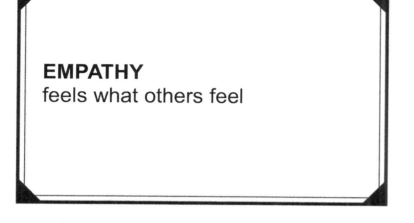

EMPATHY
feels what others feel

HOW CAN I GROW & NURTURE THIS POWER IN:

MYSELF?

OTHERS?

MY COMMUNITY?

Engagement

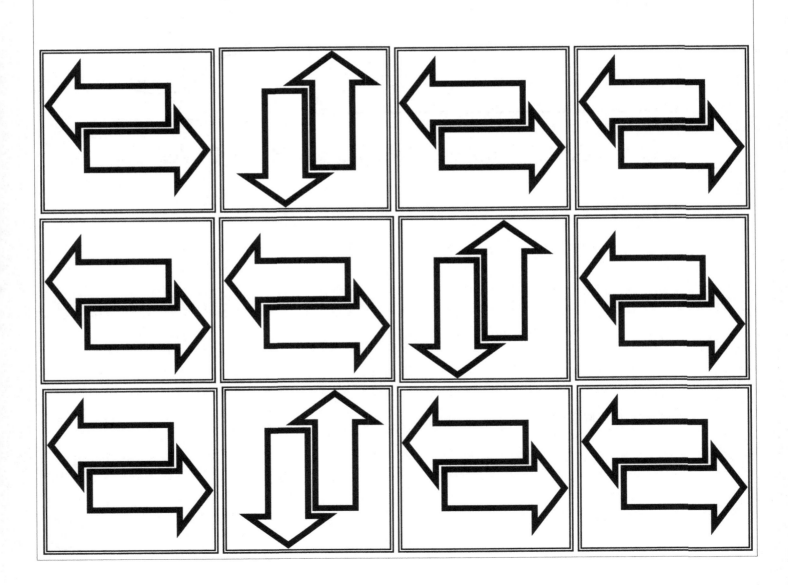

ENGAGEMENT
interacts with things and/or
people across environments

HOW CAN I GROW & NURTURE THIS POWER IN:

MYSELF?

OTHERS?

MY COMMUNITY?

Fairness

FAIRNESS
ensures equality without discrimination

HOW CAN I GROW & NURTURE THIS POWER IN:

MYSELF?

OTHERS?

MY COMMUNITY?

35

Forgiveness

FORGIVENESS
acknowledges wrongdoing without seeking revenge or punishment

HOW CAN I GROW & NURTURE THIS POWER IN:

MYSELF?

OTHERS?

MY COMMUNITY?

Gratitude

GRATITUDE
expresses and shows thanks
for things given or
benefited from

HOW CAN I GROW & NURTURE THIS POWER IN:

MYSELF?

OTHERS?

MY COMMUNITY?

Honesty

HONESTY
acts and speaks from one's
truth and with integrity

HOW CAN I GROW & NURTURE THIS POWER IN:

MYSELF?

OTHERS?

MY COMMUNITY?

HOPE
shows optimism despite
human hardships

HOW CAN I GROW & NURTURE THIS POWER IN:

MYSELF?

OTHERS?

MY COMMUNITY?

43

Humor

HUMOR
approaches life with
playfulness and lightheartedness

HOW CAN I GROW & NURTURE THIS POWER IN:

MYSELF?

OTHERS?

MY COMMUNITY?

Kindness

KINDNESS
helpful, generous, and
unconditional approach
to self and others

HOW CAN I GROW & NURTURE THIS POWER IN:

MYSELF?

OTHERS?

MY COMMUNITY?

LOVE
affection and devotion for
self and all living things

HOW CAN I GROW & NURTURE THIS POWER IN:

MYSELF?

OTHERS?

MY COMMUNITY?

Love of Learning

LOVE of LEARNING
orientation and openness to
new knowledge and
new experiences

HOW CAN I GROW & NURTURE THIS POWER IN:

MYSELF?

OTHERS?

MY COMMUNITY?

51

Patience

PATIENCE
remains steady and calm
during personal discomfort

HOW CAN I GROW & NURTURE THIS POWER IN:

MYSELF?

OTHERS?

MY COMMUNITY?

Persistence

PERSISTENCE
continues or finishes what
is started, despite difficulty,
distractions, and challenges

HOW CAN I GROW & NURTURE THIS POWER IN:

MYSELF?

OTHERS?

MY COMMUNITY?

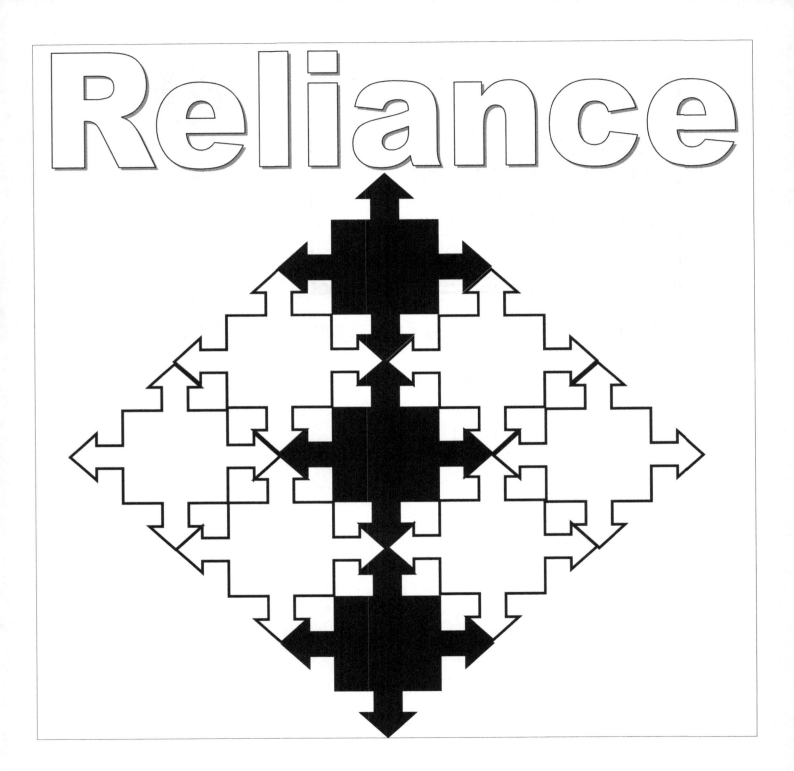

RELIANCE
recognizes interdependence
with others and the environment

HOW CAN I GROW & NURTURE THIS POWER IN:

MYSELF?

OTHERS?

MY COMMUNITY?

Resilience

RESILIENCE
capacity to recover
from adversity

HOW CAN I GROW & NURTURE THIS POWER IN:

MYSELF?

OTHERS?

MY COMMUNITY?

Responsibility

RESPONSIBILITY
accepts ownership of
one's actions

HOW CAN I GROW & NURTURE THIS POWER IN:

MYSELF?

OTHERS?

MY COMMUNITY?

Self-regulation

SELF-REGULATION

shows discretion in one's thoughts, emotions, and actions

HOW CAN I GROW & NURTURE THIS POWER IN:

MYSELF?

OTHERS?

MY COMMUNITY?

Teamwork

TEAMWORK
works effectively with others
to achieve mutual goals

HOW CAN I GROW & NURTURE THIS POWER IN:

MYSELF?

OTHERS?

MY COMMUNITY?

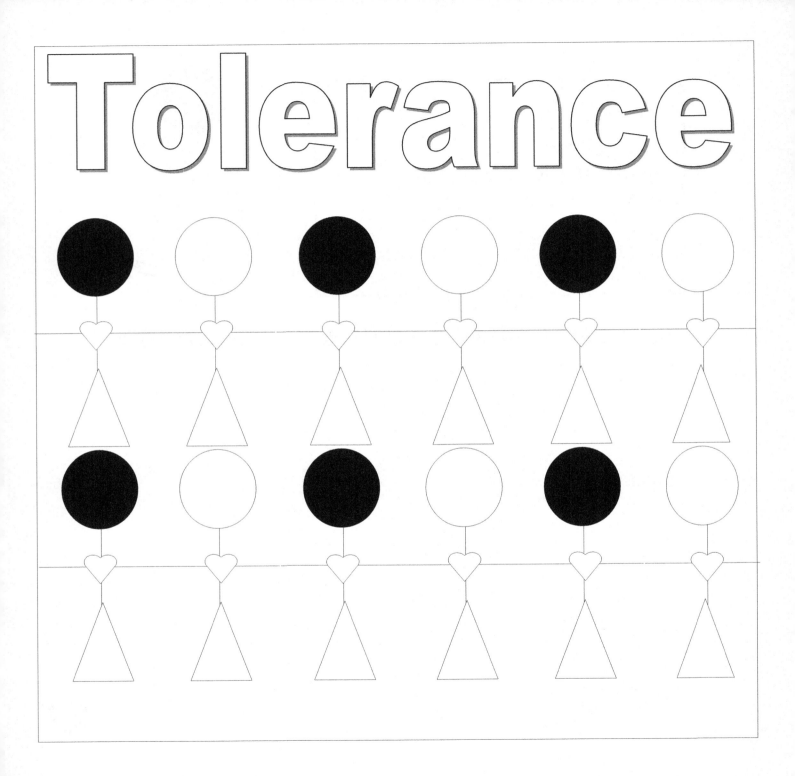

TOLERANCE
fair and objective attitude
toward differences in others

HOW CAN I GROW & NURTURE THIS POWER IN:

MYSELF?

OTHERS?

MY COMMUNITY?

67

TRUST
belief in and reliance on objects, self, and others

HOW CAN I GROW & NURTURE THIS POWER IN:

MYSELF?

OTHERS?

MY COMMUNITY?

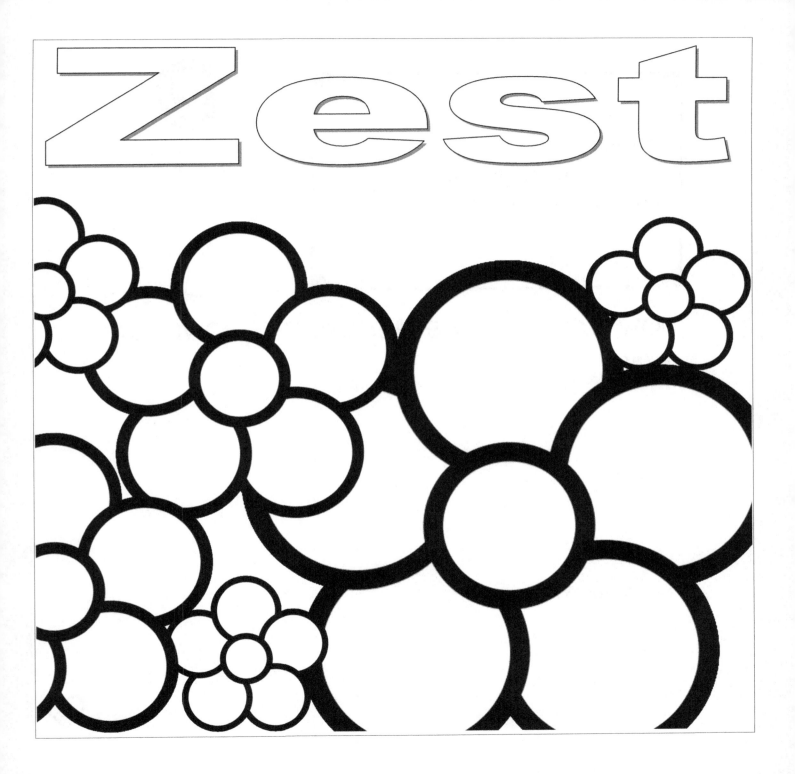

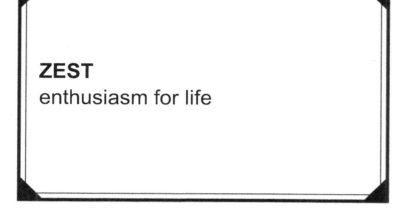

ZEST
enthusiasm for life

HOW CAN I GROW & NURTURE THIS POWER IN:

MYSELF?

OTHERS?

MY COMMUNITY?

ABOUT THE AUTHORS

Educator, writer and publisher, **Mayra Porrata,** works to promote individual and community flourishing. Her career spans the fields of business, public health, leadership development, higher education and publishing.

For ten years, Mayra taught at the School of Health Sciences at Kent State University, and also served as adjunct faculty at the Weatherhead School of Management at Case Western Reserve University.

Mayra is the founder of Soul Publishing Group™ and the author and co-author of more than a dozen titles and courses that promote a deeper understanding of our individual and shared humanity.

ABOUT THE AUTHORS

An accomplished author, sought-after consultant, and educator's educator, **Dr. Kristie Pretti-Frontczak** spent 16 years as a tenured professor in Higher Education at Kent State University before leaving to lead a {r}evolution in early childhood education.

Through comprehensive classes, thought-provoking keynote addresses, and practical resources for teachers, she's guiding adult professionals who work with our youngest students toward developing their emotional intelligence, reclaiming children's right to learn through play and reimagining more inclusive classrooms.

She has written six textbooks, two workbooks, and the AEPS curricular system, served as past President of the International Division for Early Childhood of the Council for Exceptional Children, and spent over 50,000 hours teaching adults best practices in early childhood care and education in locations from Cincinnati to Singapore. It's all part of her effort to build kinder, more inclusive, and more creative classrooms-and therefore, a better world.